LOOKING BACK AT
Chorlton~cum~Hardy
Martledge, Barlow Moor and Hough End

John Lloyd

Willow Publishing 1985
Willow Cottage, 36 Moss Lane,
Timperley, Altrincham,
Cheshire, WA15 6SZ

ISBN 0 946361 14 2

Printed by The Commercial
Centre Ltd., Clowes Street,
Hollinwood, Oldham.

Introduction

Until the mid-nineteenth century Chorlton was a rural backwater. Its population was small, 84 in 1642 had risen only to 619 in 1811, and was purely agricultural in character. It maintained itself, provided a share of the needs of neighbouring Manchester and took pride in the reflected glory of

Author's note:

All the photographs used in this album are from my own collection. With nearly 500 photographs to choose from the choice has been far from easy but it is hoped that the selection will afford pleasure to the browser.

To acknowledge the source of each picture used is not possible and it must suffice to tender a sincere 'thank you' to my many friends who have found these and continue to find new ones even now.

(Right)
The complement of Law and Order officers pose for their group photograph outside Beech Road Police Station. Tantalisingly the date of the City Sessions notice cannot be read but the recruiting enamel sign above it lasted into the 1930's. This suggests that the date was about 1925.

its two aristocratic families, the Barlows and the Mosleys, who had lived within its boundaries. Most of the recorded early history of Chorlton is that of these two families.

That is not to suggest that Chorlton is of relatively recent foundation. The names of the four segments clearly indicate their Anglo-Saxon origins, probably indicating the expansion of the main settlement of WITEGE's TUN (Withington). Chorlton itself probably stems from CEORLA-TUN, the settlement of the ceorls (a ceorl was the lowest level of Saxon freemen) although there is a counter suggestion that it was CEORLFRIP's'-TUN though we know nothing of Ceorlfrip. Hardy, that area south of Chorlton Brook was ARD-EEA, the trees (= wood) near the water (i.e. the flood plain of the Mersey (MAERES-EEA = Boundary water). Martledge, the 'New Village' to Seymour Grove was MAERES-LAACHE, the pools near the boundary and Hough End, the fourth part, was HOF-ENDE, the area or 'quarter' in which the house of the lord (= Hof) was situated. It was a vague area, much of it moss-land stretching away towards Withington and had housed the original Manor House of Withington (the Hough or, earlier, Hof situated near the present Princess Hotel) as well as the later and still existing Hough End Hall. The original house became a farm and was later replaced by Chorlton's Farm but the moat which surrounded the site remained until the present estate was built. Hough End seems to have been associated more with Withington than Chorlton after the Protestation of 1641 probably because it was more convenient to organise that enquiry from there. Chorlton as latterly defined, after the loss of Hough End, was a long narrow north to south area and constituted the most westerly part of the ancient Manor of Withington whose boundaries not only included Didsbury, Levenshulme and Gorton but stretched away to Denton and far off Haughton. It was included in the Thirty Townships of the Medieval Parish of Manchester although until after 1850 there was little enough to justify that distinction.

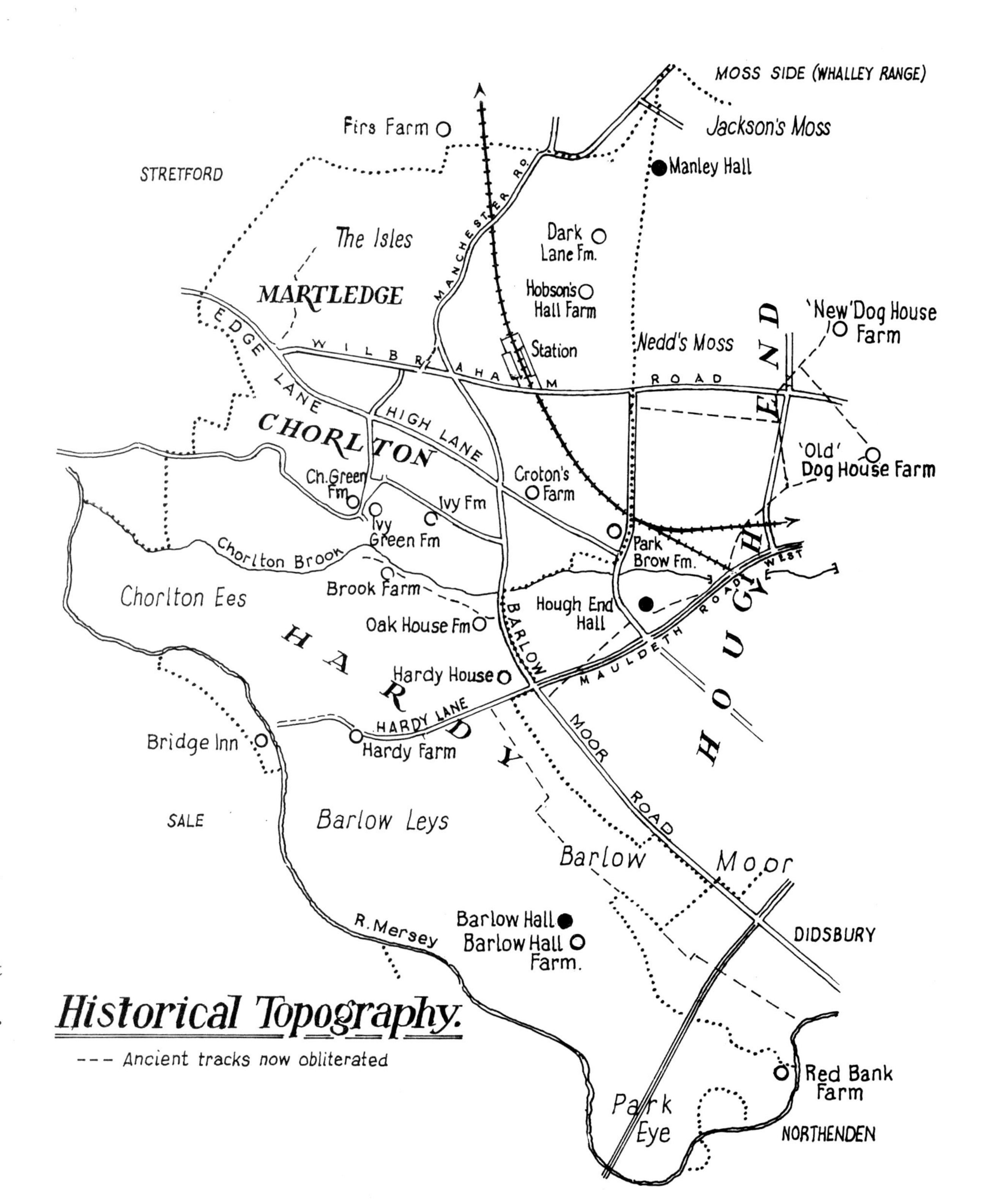

Historical Topography.

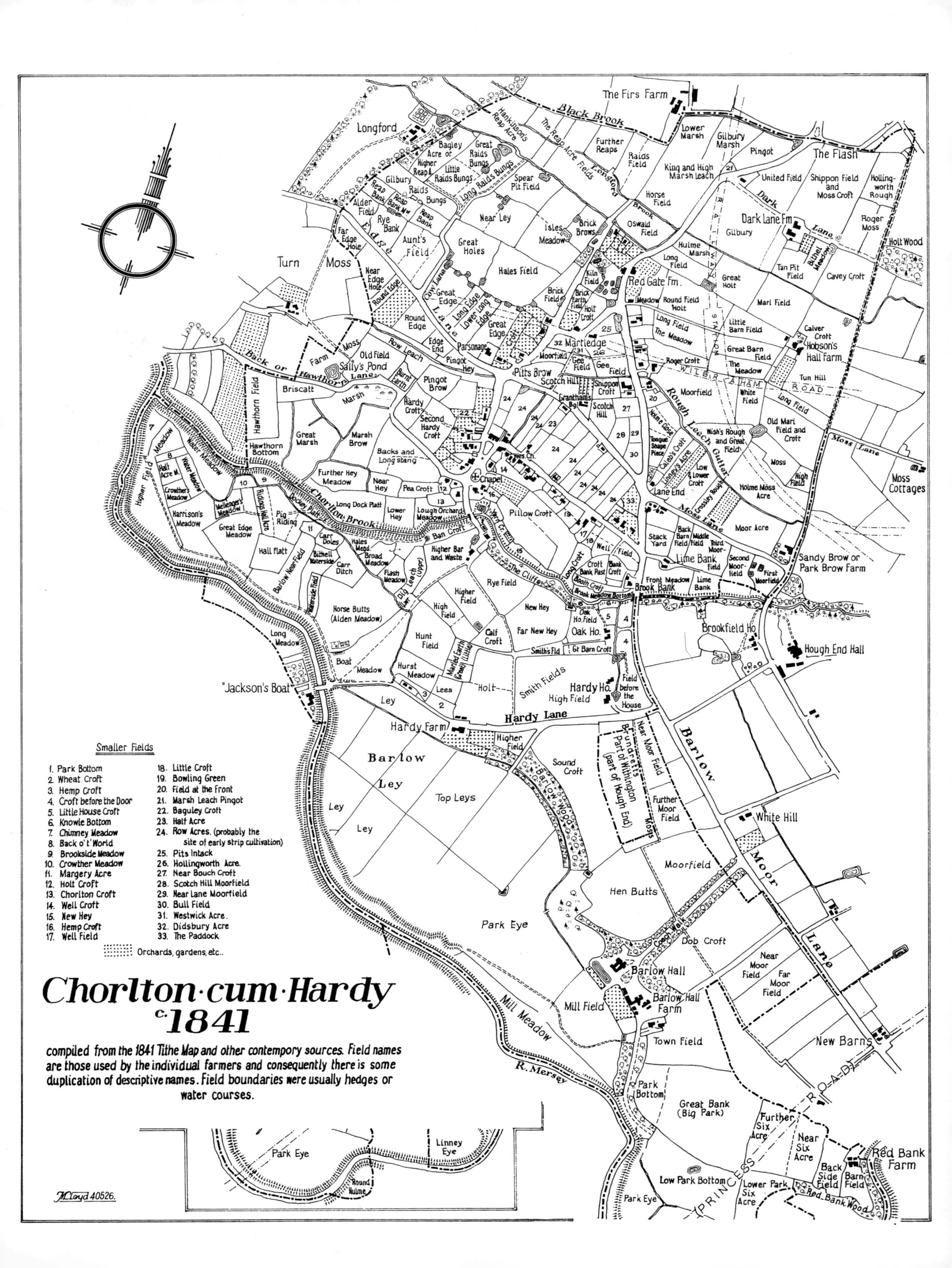
Chorlton·cum·Hardy
c.1841
compiled from the 1841 Tithe Map and other contempory sources. Field names are those used by the individual farmers and consequently there is some duplication of descriptive names. Field boundaries were usually hedges or water courses.
Smaller Fields
1. Park Bottom
2. Wheat Croft
3. Hemp Croft
4. Croft before the Door
5. Little House Croft
6. Knowle Bottom
7. Chimney Meadow
8. Back o' t' World
9. Brookside Meadow
10. Crowther Meadow
11. Margery Acre
12. Holt Croft
13. Chorlton Croft
14. Well Croft
15. New Hey
16. Hemp Croft
17. Well Field
18. Little Croft
19. Bowling Green
20. Field at the Front
21. Marsh Leach Pingot
22. Baguley Croft
23. Half Acre
24. Row Acres. (probably the site of early strip cultivation)
25. Pits Intack
26. Hollingworth Acre.
27. Near Bouch Croft
28. Scotch Hill Moorfield
29. Near Lane Moorfield
30. Bull Field
31. Westwick Acre.
32. Didsbury Acre
33. The Paddock
Orchards, gardens, etc..
The Firs Farm
Black Brook
Longford
The Flash
Dark Lane Fm
Red Gate Fm.
Hobson's Hall Farm
Moss Cottages
Sandy Brow or Park Brow Farm
Hough End Hall
Brookfield Ho.
Hardy Ho.
Hardy Lane
Hardy Farm
Barlow Moor Lane
White Hill
Barlow Hall
Barlow Hall Farm
New Barns
Red Bank Farm
Princess Road
"Jackson's Boat"
Chorlton Brook
R. Mersey
Chapel
Wilbraham Road
Turn Moss
Park Eye
M. Lloyd 40526.

The Mosleys and Hough End

The Moseley family came to Manchester from Moseley near Wolverhampton. By 1465 one Jenkyn Moseley was living at the Hough. The present Hough End Hall was built for Nicholas Mosley in 1596 but it seems probable that there was an earlier house on this site. Whether this was the home of Jenkyn or, as the Longfords who were the Lords of the Manor at the time lived at Longford in Derbyshire, he lived at the original Manor House is not known. Nicholas acting in association with his brother Anthony of Ancoats went to London and became a very successful merchant in the best Dick Whittington tradition. He became a favourite of Elizabeth I and had his new house built to retire to and died there in 1612.

Sir Nicholas, his knighthood was bestowed on him in recognition of services rendered, changed the family name from Moseley to Mosley in order to pun with the motto he adopted with the grant of arms which went with his knighthood.

His grandson was a staunch Royalist and was actively concerned with the Civil War. His adherence to this cause resulted in the granting of a baronetcy by Charles I and the impoverishment of his family. The Mosley association with Chorlton ended as a result of the marriage in Chorlton Chapel in 1685 of Anne to Sir John Bland. In two generations the various estates had been sold off to pay off debts incurred by Sir John, their son and two grandsons. The lands in Chorlton were bought by Samuel Egerton of Tatton and George Lloyd of Yorkshire.

Sir Nicholas's new house was attractively built of locally made brick with stone facings. The oldest existing picture shows it to have been free of the clutter of outbuildings and lean-to's which were later to have disfigured it as a farm.

While functioning as a farm it was commonly known as Peacock Farm from the birds of that species which strutted about in the front yard.

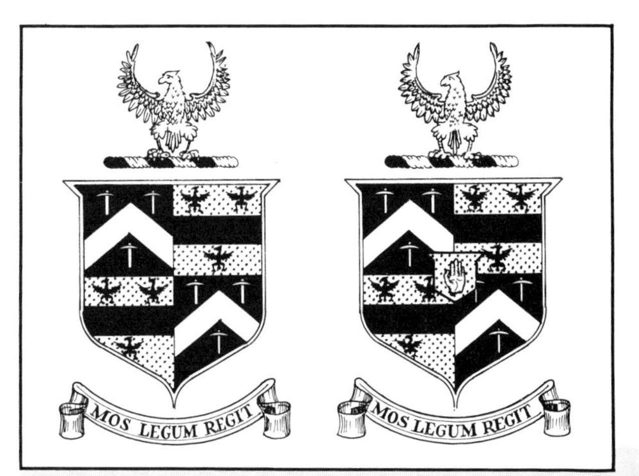

(Left)
Arms of Sir Nicholas Mosley 1527–1612.

(Right)
Arms of Sir Edward Mosley, Baronet, 1616–57. This was used as the badge of the Withington Urban District Council and more recently by the Burnage Grammar School.

Hough End Hall

The south-west corner of Hough End Hall about 1885. The night door is clearly shown and from the room above the small circular window permitted the servant on duty to see the approach of returning members of the household along the straight drive from Barlow Moor Lane. It was usual in such cases to have a trap in the floor of the room so that he could drop down and have the door open for their arrival. The approach drive is still perpetuated by the path across the Park.

The Hall about 1932 before the building of the school. The disfigurement caused by the buildings necessary to its function as a farm is clearly shown. There were other outbuildings behind the trees on the right.

The Barlows of Barlow Hall

The Barlow family came to the district sometime in the thirteenth century. The family originated near Barlow in Derbyshire where they were neighbours of the ancient family of d'Abitot which had marriage ties with the Longfords and Grelleys (Lords of the Manors of Withington and Manchester respectively). The Grelleys (or Gresleys) were a branch of the Albini family of Seale (near Burton-on-Trent) who also held lands in Salford Hundred.

Alexander d'Albini settled his land in Salford Hundred on Thomas de Barlow in return for his service which was acknowledged by the giving of two pairs of white gloves at Christmas. This was just before the end of the century and within the reign of Edward I (1272–1307) Sir Robert de Barlow had taken up residence at Barlow Hall. The foregoing is given in order to explain the origin of the place name Barlow and dispel the oft quoted statement that Sale in Cheshire was involved.

Nothing is known of the original hall. It was probably very simple and would be extended and improved as time went on. The building was certainly extensively rebuilt in 1584 and this might well have been the basic house which was much damaged by fire in 1879. The Barlows were staunch Catholics, the Mosleys equally staunch Protestants. The oft quoted story of an underground tunnel linking the two houses is therefore obviously false on this count alone, though there are other reasons.

The most famous of the Barlows was, without doubt, Edward (chr. 1585) who became Father Ambrose and was executed at Lancaster in 1641. He was recently beatified by the Roman Catholic Church. The family came to an end with the death of Thomas in 1773. The estate was bought by the Egertons of Tatton and subsequent tenants of the Hall included Thomas Walker the great political reformer, Stephen Philips and William Cunliffe Brooks.

(Left)
The arms of the Barlows of Co. Lancashire had little in common with other branches of the family but much similarity to those of their patron the d'Albinis. This was a common form of acknowledgement.

(Above)
The west front of Barlow Hall about the turn of the century. At this time the alterations which so altered the appearance of the frontage had not been carried out.

(Below middle)

The Courtyard with the sundial and its motto: 'Lumen me regit, ves umbra' (I am guided by the sun, you by the shade). The window of the private chapel is on the left.

(Below left)

The 'Sitting Room' with its stained-glass panels of family related arms. It is probable that this was originally the family's private chapel.

(Right)

The tenants of Barlow Hall seem to have bestowed their patronage on all sorts of local organisations. Chorlton Prize Brass Band were invited in 1893 and had their photograph taken with the west front as the backcloth.

(Below right)

The Estate Bell of Barlow Hall which would be familiar to Edward Barlow (Father Ambrose) now hangs in the nearby St. Ambrose's Church and is used in the celebration of the Mass.

Chorlton Churches

It is generally accepted that the first church, or rather chapel of Chorlton was erected about 1512 probably by the Barlows and in its early years would see the celebration of the Roman Mass. There is an 18th-century Article of Enquiry in the Cheshire Record Office which states that the chapel was built in the last year of the reign of King Henry IV (c.1412) and rebuilt about the 10th year of King Henry VIII. This evidence should not be accepted without reservation and be it as it might the generally agreed building is that shown here.

It was a small but very attractive half-timbered building on a stone foundation; Denton Parish Church still stands as a fine example of the same style. This first church was life expired after 250 years and was replaced in 1779/80 by a very plain rectangular brick structure. A growing population made it necessary to undertake enlargement in 1837 by the addition of two side aisles. In this form it served the community for over a hundred years although it received a number of additions and improvements particularly by the benevolence of Mr. Brooks and Sam Mendel. A Chapel of Ease, the 'New Church' was provided to cater for the ever growing and socially aloof congregation but it did not become the Parish Church until the 'Old Church' was closed in 1940 as a result of frost damage. This was to lead to its ultimate demolition in 1949.

The first challenge to the Established Church came about 1770 when Wesleyan Methodism was introduced. The first services were held in the houses of various adherents and in the barn, which still stands, of the Higginbottom family. The zeal of the members led to the building of their first chapel in Beech Road in 1805 but a larger building was needed by 1827. A meeting room was built, which still stands as the Beech Inn, for use as a day and Sunday school as well as other activities but due to a legal technicality the ownership of the building was lost. A new Chapel in Manchester Road was necessary by 1873.

(Below)
The first chapel of 1512 from the south.

(Right)
The 'Old' Parish Church about 1880 before the addition of the north porch.

Industrial and commercial Manchester was expanding rapidly and many of the families connected with this growth took up residence in Chorlton. The result was a rapid increase in the number of churches and chapels of different denominations which were founded. The Macfadyan Congregational Church was established in 1879 followed by the Unitarian Chapel in 1901, the Macpherson Memorial Primitive Methodist in 1902 and the Presbyterian Church of England in 1903. In the meantime the Parish of St. Werburgh had been carved out of several parishes including St. Clement's. One result of the influx of wealthy families was a huge increase in the number of servants employed. Many of them came from Ireland and soon they formed a considerable Catholic congregation. The Catholic Parish of St. Augustine was formed in 1890 and a Priory was established where Needham Avenue now is. When the Priory was closed the centre of the Parish was established on High Lane in premises which had been the Chorlton Commercial School and which in its turn gave way to a new church and the new parochial title of St. John in 1927.

The spate of new churches at the start of the century was continued with the McLaren Baptist Church in 1907 and the Emmanuel Free Church in 1909. Many of these places of worship are now closed and demolished but there have been others to replace them but it is not within the ambit of this book to record them here.

4 Wesleyan Chapel, Beech Road

6 Augustinian Priory

5 Wesleyan Chapel, Manchester Road

1 Old Church

3 Macfadyen Memorial Congregational Church

2 Macpherson Primitive Methodist Church

1
The interior of the Old Church probably about 1910. The east window was the gift of Mr. Brooks.

2
The Macpherson Primitive Methodist Church in High Lane. The nearer building was the school and it still stands.

3
The Macfadyen Memorial Congregational Church about 1900. The nearer building was the school and was built first and used as the church until the church proper was built. The church is now demolished and the school has reverted to its dual role.

4
The second (1827) Wesleyan Methodist Chapel in Beech Road. The building still stands but has been reduced in height. The first chapel occupied the graveyard between the present building and the road. On the right can be seen the path leading to the three cottages of which the nearest was the original Trevor Arms Hotel.

5
A contemporary engraving of the third Wesleyan Chapel in Manchester Road which was opened in 1873.

6
The Augustinian Priory which stood where Needham Avenue and Priory Avenue now are. It looked like exactly what it was, a secular house (called 'Oakley' and originally built in 1835) used for religious purposes.

Chorlton Schools

Reference has already been made to the opening of the first day school in Chorlton by the Methodists. The Church of England did not build their school on the Green until 1845. By 1878 it had been condemned as inadequate by the Board of Education's Inspectors and a new and larger building replaced it in 1879. The layout was as simple as the curriculum, a small room for infants, a larger room for the older pupils and a small side room for the 'top class'. As the writer remembers it in 1920 it still had cockspur gas jets for lighting, coal fires and slates were still used.

After the 'New School' was built in St. Clement's Road in 1901 the 'Old School' catered for infants and juniors but eventual improvements in local education made it redundant and today it serves other uses.

The explosion in the population of Chorlton towards the turn of the century resulted in the establishment of a considerable number of private schools. The children of the new generation of Chorltonians were not, seemingly, encouraged to mix with the rough element of Old Chorltonians so the demand was quickly satisfied by maiden ladies anxious to exchange their expertise in gracious living for pin-money and scholastics like Robert Davies who established Chorlton Commercial Schools (sic) in 1872 and Charles Dadley's Chorlton Grammer School in 1896.

The arts were an essential element in the upbringing of the families of gentlemen and were amply catered for by private schools of music, dancing and art.

When Manchester absorbed Withington U.D.C. (of which Chorlton was a part) in 1904 it was necessary to augment the public education facilities for by this time the upper classes (!) were already moving further from the City as transport facilities improved and those from nearer the centre who took their place were increasingly dependent on the local authority for such services. As an interim measure Tom Mostyn's Art School was pressed into service while a temporary school was erected at the corner of Oswald and Nicolas Roads. At the same time a permanent school of standard 'School Board' design was built next to it and opened in April 1909. The temporary building became Chorlton Central School and a temporary infants school of the same type of construction in Sandy Lane was never so used and became the initial unit of Chorlton High School in 1924.

(Below left)
The first Church of England School on the Green. It was replaced in 1879 by the larger building shown below. The schoolmaster's house was a feature of both buildings.

(Below right)
There was a suggestion, for which the drawings exist, for increasing the capacities of this later building by adding another floor but the school in St. Clement's Road was built instead.

(Bottom right)

Tom Mostyn's Art School after it had been taken over as Chorlton's first municipal school. It is still recognisable though now it is the headquarters of the Road Transport Union.

(Right middle)

A photograph of about 1925 of Oswald Road Municipal Elementary School

(Below left)

The Central School used a house in Keppel Road as a housecraft centre.

(Right)

C. C. Dadley, M.A., provided a Grammar School which specialised in training for 'Law, Medical, Accountants Prelims, University, Civil Services Exams &c.' according to the board outside. The house on the corner of High Lane and Stockton Road still stands but no longer serves as a school.

(Below right)

Typical of the private schools was 'Springfield' on the corner of Barlow Moor Road and Napier Road. Older boys went to Mr. Dadley or schools away from home for they were all for 'Girls and Junior Boys'. Earlier this house, with that behind it in Napier Road, had been Mr. Dadley's Grammar School.

Chorlton's Public Houses

A great deal of deep study will be necessary before anything like a dependable record can be compiled of the licenced houses of Chorlton. With the complications which come from there being no addresses in the records (in a place like Chorlton addresses were superfluous), the anonymity which often accompanied those beerhouses licenced under the 1830 legislation and the ease with which a name could be changed at the whim of a landlord or taken with him as a sort of trade mark when he moved, it is unlikely that a positive record will ever be established.

The Bowling Green Hotel is reputed to have been licenced in 1693 though the Recognizance list of 1780 only records the Bay Horse and the White Lion. This pair had been joined by the Horse & Jockey by 1783 and the White Lion had disappeared by 1786. The White Lion is at the present a mystery but the Bay Horse may have been the house in Sandy Lane (then Moss Lane) which had a licence in 1832 under the sign of the Black Horse and which was closed by the magistrates about 1870 for persistent offences against the restrictive Sunday Licencing Laws.

The house at Jackson's Boat, until recently properly known as the Bridge Inn and before that as The Old Greyhound is said to have been there before 1760 when it was used, probably because of its remoteness, as a meeting place for Jacobite sympathisers. George Jackson 'of the boate' signed the Protestation of 1641 and his son, presumably, married Isabell Barlow in 1681.

Coming to more recent times Ellwood refers to a small beerhouse on Nell Lane on the site of Eliza Mellor's house. This was near to the present Southern Hotel. A reference in the South Manchester Chronicle of 21st August 1891 reported that it was known as the Royal Oak and the sign was transferred to a new house on Barlow Moor Road in 1819.

By the turn of the century the Bridge, Bowling Green, Horse & Jockey, Beech, Trevor Arms, Traveller's Rest and Royal Oak had been joined by the Lloyd Platt and the Oaks. This latter, opposite Southern Cemetery gates was unashamedly built to catch the trade from the crowds which flocked to the Cemetery and made it into a major popular attraction.

(Above)

The Green end of Beech Road about 1900. On the right is the ornamental lamp over the door of the old Trevor Arms Hotel and on the left is that of the Traveller's Rest. Mr. Neale, the butcher, passes the time of day with a youth on a horse without fear of the danger from traffic!

(Above left)

The Bridge Inn about 1910 with the custodian of the gate showing interest in Mr. Neil (the photographer). When the inn was cut off by floods a barrel of beer would be available in a bedroom in case somebody in a boat called for a drink during 'hours'. This was no joke but safeguarded the licence at a time when the Law recognised no justification for not supplying refreshment when legally permitted. The 'teetotal' element were not above using such a situation to cause a hostelry to lose its licence.

(Above right)

The original 1816 footbridge over the Mersey. By the time this photograph was taken in 1865 the centre support had been washed away and in 1880 that on the Chorlton side also went. The replacement bridge was opened on 14th October 1881 but it is recorded that the original was washed away a few hours before.

(Right)

The nineteenth-century Bowling Green Hotel. It would seem that this building dates from about 1780 and was the second licenced house on the site.

(Below left)
The replacement house built in 1908. Though not very old, this photograph is already historic in view of the refurbishment of the property.

(Left)
The bowling green behind the old house shown above. In the centre is Mrs. Alice Lythgoe, the licencee's wife, on the right is Tom Lythgoe, her husband and his partner Tom Dean.

(Below right)
The old Royal Oak dating from 1819. This house had associations with the murder of P.C. Cock by Charles Peace. The need to avoid any lapse in opening to preserve the licence meant that usually replacement buildings were built alongside the old so that at the due time there was no interruption in the service. In the case of the Royal Oak as there was no space available at the side the new building was built round the old which was then demolished inside.

(Right)
The Horse & Jockey about 1895. The building jutting out on the right was Miss Wilton's out-house and behind it is her cottage.

(Below)
The Horse & Jockey about 1928. The 'black and white' was applied about 1907/08. Miss Wilton's cottage has been incorporated into the pub but the raised section at the far end still shows the raised doorway which was reached by a flight of outside steps. It was in this part of the building that Miss Wilton held a private school and which no doubt gives rise to the oft repeated story that the Horse & Jockey was originally (i.e. before it was a pub) a school.

Entertainment

The 'New Chorltonians' patronised the theatres and concert halls of Manchester or indulged in the many cultural and educational institutions they had established. The 'Old Chorltonians' were content with an occasional concert in the schoolroom or the Reading-room on Beech Road. From time to time the conscience of the newcomers would be stirred and they would discharge their social obligations to the elderly with a tasteful selection of renderings, both musical and recited, tea and cakes, a screw of tobacco for the men and a half-a-crown for the women and a couple or so speeches designed to be uplifting and to leave no doubt as to the source of the bounty.

Came the new century and the bioscope promised to bring cheap and exciting entertainment to all – which really meant the poorer of the community. At first these shows were nothing more than a fairground sideshow but as premises became available to house the equipment and the audience, they became more permanent.

One of these early 'palaces' was housed in a corrugated iron mission church on Clarendon Road which had become redundant when a permanent chapel was built on Egerton Road. Another was on the corner of Oswald Road and Longford Road where the newer houses are, in the dip, and catered for a variety of activities including roller skating under the name of The Longford Picturedrome. No photographs have been found of either but a very nice one of The Chorlton Pavilion and Winter Gardens has survived. It provided stage entertainment as well as the moving pictures and survived until after the first war. Chorlton eventually had three purpose built cinemas. The oldest was the Palais-de-Luxe, opened 1915, and now a supermarket; the Majestic/Savoy/Gaumont/A.B.C. is now an undertakers establishment and the Rivoli/Essoldo/Classic of 1937 which is now a cycle dealers showroom.

(Left)
The narrow strip of land on the east side of the railway from Chorlton Junction through to Throstle Nest was intended for quadrupling the railway tracks. Consequently only building of a temporary nature was permitted. The bill-board advertises 'The Whips' which was probably a concert party for the week commencing Monday 20th June, 1910. It is recorded that Wee Georgie Wood played here as a child and was required to attend Oswald Road School. In 1909 the Pavilion became the first theatre in the H.D.M. circuit owned by a local Manchester solicitor, H. D. Moorhouse.

(Above left)
The Savoy cinema about 1931. In spite of the name Majestic appearing on the face of the building it was known as the Savoy from its opening with that name covering up the original. 'With Cobham to the Cape' and 'The Perfect Clown' with Larry Semon are billed.

(Above right)
The front of the Palais-de-Luxe with its glass canopy is seen in the centre of this picture of the 'Tram Terminus'. The front was of glazed tiles in green and white and the two round windows looked not unlike huge eyes.

Events

Chorlton's rapid translation from a sparsely populated and scattered agricultural community to suburban status meant that it missed out on many things that other nearby communities regarded as normal. In spite of the shops in Beech Road being in the Market Place (according to the stone inscription over the butchers) no details of the functioning of that institution have come down to us. When Chorlton did achieve a market hall (about 1930?) it got two! One was about halfway down Longford Road and was so small that in a short time it became a decorator's workshop and the other by the bridge over the brook on Barlow Moor Road did not last much longer. It is now a part of the same cycle sales organisation as the old cinema next door.

Similarly there have been occasional attempts to promote a carnival but be it market or carnival the aloofness on the importee Chorltonians of a hundred years ago seems to still exercise its influence.

The biggest popular demonstration was the St. Clement's Annual Procession of Witness. This was the sole surviving remnant of the old wakes which was observed in the week following the third Sunday in July. Some other churches mounted small processions but the Parish Church's gathering on the Green, the prayers and the traditional singing of the Old Hundredth followed by a procession round the Parish was the highlight of the religious year. No longer is the custom observed. Perhaps traffic conditions made it too dangerous for the children, perhaps it inconvenienced the motorist or perhaps new thinking decided it was archaic.

From time to time the past is revived for shoppers when the Morris Men perform though, let it be said, whilst Chorlton in the past had Mummers, Lifters, Bands of various types and honoured many old customs, I have never seen reference to a ring of Morris Men.

(Top)
St. Clement's Procession of Witness leaving the Green in 1938. Right up to the end of the Old Church the distinction between the adherents of each church was clearly marked.

(Inset)
Chorlton Prize Band was a traditional element in the procession as long as it could muster sufficient members. It is shown here in 1937 as it left the Green towards Hawthorn Road.

(Above left)
Participants in a Chorlton Carnival of the mid-30s passing along Oswald Road. Attempts to organise these events seemed usually to be centred in this part of Chorlton.

(Above right)
An important tradition in the sporting calendar was the holding of charity bowling tournaments on the greens of the Bowling Green and the Lloyd-Platt Hotels. This photograph shows contestants on the green at the Bowling Green but the date and the charity being supported is not recorded.

Chorlton Green

There are no early records of Chorlton Green. If we apply the patterns of change which are widespread in England where common land, roadside verges and the like are involved, we can be reasonably sure of what happened in the past though not necessarily when with any degree of certainty.

Encroachment is the description of the taking over of common land without legal title and with practically the whole of the Township in the ownership of two families (one of them being Lords of the Manor) it would probably go by default.

It would be reasonable then to suggest that the piece of common land from which the Green emerged was much larger than the area of today. It would extend from the rear building line of the old brewery of the Horse & Jockey to the Brook and, similarly from the entry behind Zetland Terrace and the old National School to the houses and farms on the west side. The first Chapel (1512) built on the flood terrace to avoid flooding effectively contained the area on the south and the original building (of which the present Horse & Jockey is the descendant and said to be roughly contemporary with the Chapel) further restricted the site on the north. The first Church School was built on land earlier occupied by a cottage and barn which was probably in itself an encroachment. Whether Higginbottom's Chorlton Green Farm and the one now used as a motor mechanics were built on land that had been part of the common land is uncertain but there seems little doubt that the barn which restricts the exit from the Green to Brookburn Road was.

The site of the Chapel (it was a Chapel of Ease of the Parish Church of Manchester until the formation of the Parish of Chorlton-cum-Hardy in 1839) partitioned off an area by the village fishpond and no doubt it became very popular as the meeting place of the menfolk when the day's work was done. That it should be used for playing the ever popular game of bowls, then more akin to the present-day French game of 'boule' than 'crown green', and a convivial drink in the meantime is understandable. The Bowling Green (1693) and its green no doubt developed from the need to satisfy this demand.

The final act of encroachment came early in the last century when Samuel Wilton sometime after 1816 (for in that year he was licencee of the Old Greyhound) appropriated the triangular centre of what was left of the original common land, planted a hedge round it and made it into his garden. Miss Wilton, his daughter, died leaving no heir so the property reverted to the Lord of the Manor, by this time Lord Egerton of Tatton, who returned it to public use in 1895.

Since then it has changed but little. The drinking fountain which might well have been provided to mark the arrival of piped water in 1864 was removed to the Recreation Ground in Beech Road and seems to have disappeared from there at the time of the scrap metal drive during the last war. In recent years the gravel surface has been replaced by turf and the ornamental lamp is now in use again though using electricity instead of the gas of yesterday.

The Green with the hedge that marked it off as Miss Wilton's garden. Zetland Terrace (right background) built in 1883 dates the photograph as about 1890. To the left of the little sweet-shop (G. Green was the proprietor) is the short fence of the Maddocks' cottage's garden with the forecourt of the inn behind.

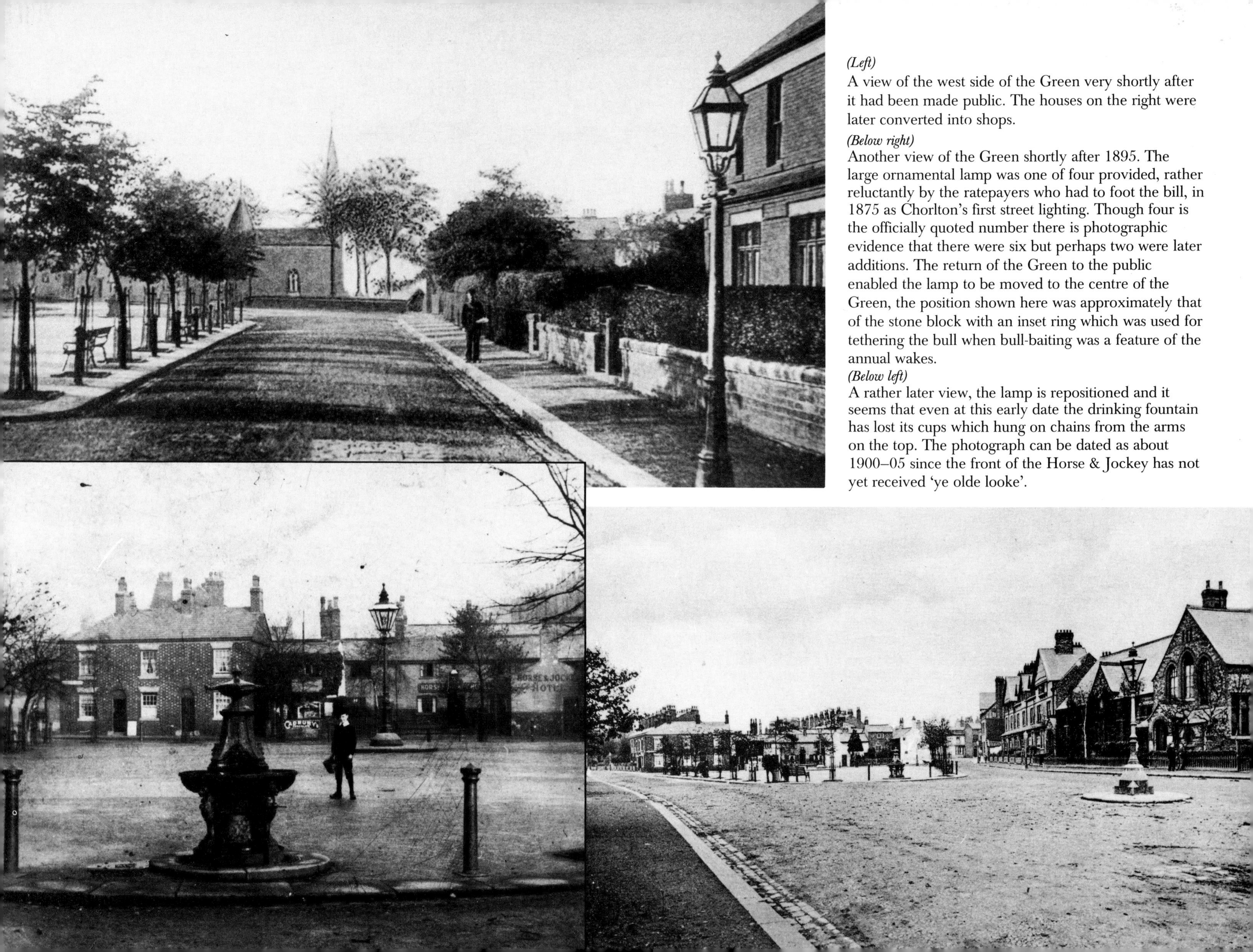

(Left)
A view of the west side of the Green very shortly after it had been made public. The houses on the right were later converted into shops.

(Below right)
Another view of the Green shortly after 1895. The large ornamental lamp was one of four provided, rather reluctantly by the ratepayers who had to foot the bill, in 1875 as Chorlton's first street lighting. Though four is the officially quoted number there is photographic evidence that there were six but perhaps two were later additions. The return of the Green to the public enabled the lamp to be moved to the centre of the Green, the position shown here was approximately that of the stone block with an inset ring which was used for tethering the bull when bull-baiting was a feature of the annual wakes.

(Below left)
A rather later view, the lamp is repositioned and it seems that even at this early date the drinking fountain has lost its cups which hung on chains from the arms on the top. The photograph can be dated as about 1900–05 since the front of the Horse & Jockey has not yet received 'ye olde looke'.

(Above)
A much more recent view taken from the popular viewpoint near the churchyard. The trees which were so small in earlier views have now grown to mature size and a telephone box stands where the drinking fountain once stood.

(Right)
There were three farms facing on to the Green of which two, though not as the farms they were, survive. The one that has gone was Ivy Green Farm, sometimes called Laburnum Cottage and latterly as Greenwood's Farm. A recent development of 'town houses' now occupies this site.

The Old Village

To most outsiders the Old Village is the Green but there is more to it than that. The importance of this part of the Township waned as the New Village developed as a result of the opening of the railway station in 1880. It has retained much of its character and from time to time finds momentary fame as a television setting.

Time has now largely eased the 'them and us' attitude that for many years estranged the two communities. Those who steadfastly proclaimed themselves Old Chorltonians are passing on while the population movements generally have resulted in a generation that never knew of the division.

A part of Chorlton which is neither the Old or New Village is that which developed along Barlow Moor Road and the 'Tram Terminus'. It seems more appropriate to put it with the Old Village for it does not have a district name of its own.

(Right)
Hyme's Cottage, Hardy Croft. The path on the right became Albermarle Road. It is recorded that this building served as Chorlton's contribution to the housing of the poor and homeless. In some sources it is referred to as the 'Almshouses' and passed to Chorlton (on Medlock) Board of Guardians.

(Below left)
At the end of Beech Road was the old established firm of T. C. Whitaker. Currants for Christmas at 4d lb., and bacon and ham hanging in the open air. But orders were delivered, to the better off, in their own pony and trap.

(Below right)
James Unsworth's butchers shop on the Green. The date is not known but about 1930 is suggested. A display of meat in the open air like this would not be tolerated now. The shop which was originally a house is now used for other purposes.

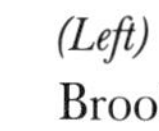

(Left)

Brook Farm stood in Brook Road and has been completely rebuilt as the Express Dairy Depot. Brook Cottage behind it was for a time used as the Curate's house. Brook Road is now Brookburn Road.

(Above left)

After the Sewage Farm was built and a system of flood control established it was usual to flood the field behind where the United Services Club stands each winter. If there was a sharp enough frost it provided a skating rink for miles around.

(Above right)

An old viewpoint probably before 1890 showing the old Parish Church from the Skating Meadow. To the left is the cottage which stood on Holt Croft on the corner of Hawthorn Road then and Ivygreen Road now.

(Above left)
Sutton's Cottage stood on the corner of Wilton Road (to the right) and Beech Road (in the foreground). It was typical of the housing of the district before the building explosion that resulted from the influx of new residents. This photograph appeared in the Wesleyan Chapel Bazaar Handbook of 1885 just before the cottage was demolished in 1891.

(Above right)
Beech Road looking towards the Market Place from near the Traveller's Call Inn. The thatched building nearer the camera is Brownhill's Saddlers shop and behind it is the Old Smithy with John Clarke, the smith, looking to see what the excitement was about. The picture dates from the 1880's.

(Right)
A rare picture of the Half Acre Field which was to become the Beech Road Recreation Ground. It was being ploughed, probably for the last time, and in the distance can be seen the roofs of Ivy Farm (left) and the new shops of the Market Place (right). The date is thought to be 1896 and the Recreation Ground was the gift of Lord Egerton to the people of Chorlton.

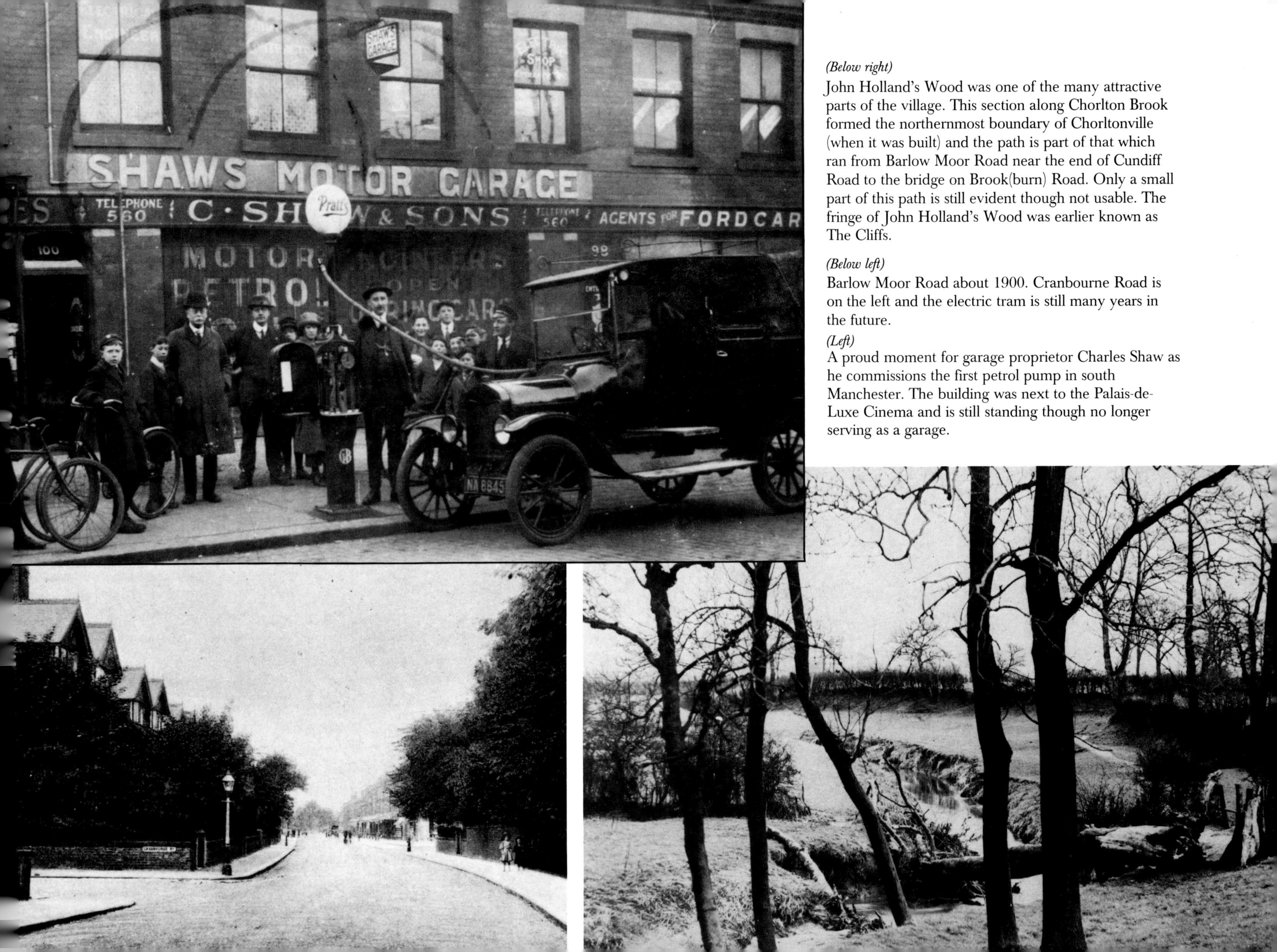

(Below right)
John Holland's Wood was one of the many attractive parts of the village. This section along Chorlton Brook formed the northernmost boundary of Chorltonville (when it was built) and the path is part of that which ran from Barlow Moor Road near the end of Cundiff Road to the bridge on Brook(burn) Road. Only a small part of this path is still evident though not usable. The fringe of John Holland's Wood was earlier known as The Cliffs.

(Below left)
Barlow Moor Road about 1900. Cranbourne Road is on the left and the electric tram is still many years in the future.

(Left)
A proud moment for garage proprietor Charles Shaw as he commissions the first petrol pump in south Manchester. The building was next to the Palais-de-Luxe Cinema and is still standing though no longer serving as a garage.

(Below right)

Beech Road from Barlow Moor Road. The gate and gatehouse to Beech House (from which the road takes its name) stood, very roughly, where the Police Station now stands. It is thought that the tree overhanging the road in the middle distance is that which bestowed its name on the residence and the road.

(Right)

Until the M63 was opened, heavy traffic through Chorlton was increasing at an alarming rate. This view dates from about 1938 and both before and after the war the heavy traffic in coal from the East Midlands to the power stations of South Lancashire presented a major hazard.

(Below left)

Croton's Farm on Sandy Lane. The story is told that old Mr. Croton bought a goose to fatten up for Christmas. It proved to be such an excellent 'watch-dog' and pet that it escaped its intended fate and served as the guardian of the farmyard for many years.

The New Village

It is not generally appreciated how many conurbations, big and small, have 'moved' in the course of the centuries. The reasons are many but the movement of the hub of Chorlton from the Green to the New Village was the common one, that development followed the building of the railway and opening of the station in 1880.

There had been an earlier movement as a result of the opening of Stretford station in 1849 but no pressure to develop a new centre emerged because the people involved were not numerically sufficient and had no need of a local shopping centre as most of their supplies came from Stretford or Manchester. The opening of Chorlton station was quite different, by this date the earlier immigrants along Edge Lane had already moved on to more distant pastures and the newer generation were more numerous and of increasingly lower social standing.

Consequently the New Village spread outwards from the station and there developed new shops and institutions like banks. Even the Post Office was coaxed away from Beech Road, at first to a compromise position on High Lane but then bowed to the inevitable and opened offices in both old and new.

It is perhaps a reflection on the characters of the two elements that the sole blacksmith remained in the Old Village and the banks were established in the New. There is still no bank (other than the Post Office Savings and Giro Bank) in the Old Village.

(Right)
A feature of developing communities up to and just after the first war was the establishment of shops by the multiple butchers, grocers, shoe shops and the Maypole Dairy Co. Chorlton's branch of the Maypole was on Wilbraham Road next to Martin's (now Barclays) Bank. Here a proud staff show off their skill at window dressing and while posters advertise tea at 1/6d (7½p) per quarter and margarine at 1/- (5p.) per lb., some of the statements would offend today's code of advertising practice.

(Above left)
From the railway bridge looking along Wilbraham Road towards Barlow Moor Road. The property between Albany Road and Keppel Road is still a terrace of large houses with front gardens. Their conversion into shops came later but a look at the scene today will show just how the conversion was carried out.

(Above right)
Wilbraham Road and Barlow Moor Road crossing about 1890. The house behind the wall is recognisable as the bank of today and the shops on the left have not changed in appearance as far as Keppel Road. The County Bank, now NatWest, was then on the corner of Albany Road and the site which it was later to occupy was still a cottage.

One could say that Chorlton Station produced the New Village. In its time when a very large part of Chorlton's male population worked in Manchester it provided their usual method of getting to work. The outside of the station was usually quiet outside rush hours but between 7 a.m. and 9 a.m. it was a scene of frantic bustle. At tea-time the homeward bound masses spread out across the road like today's football fans after a match. Many people were able to come home for their dinner! There was a ready sale for newspapers and magazines and for many years Messrs. W. H. Smith had a flourishing bookstall. In this photograph Reg Croton whose taxi waited outside (1eft) poses with the manager David Ball (right).

Photographs of the inside of the station seem not to have been very common, indeed this very heavily retouched one is the only example to turn up so far. In those days, about 1895?, there was a footbridge but this was later removed to save the expense of maintaining it and the public had to use the road bridge.

The Meadows

Until the building of the Withington Sewage Works the Ordnance Survey maps showed the area along the river as Chorlton Ees, a direct link with the Anglo-Saxon settlers from whose language the word ea meaning stream or river (and hence anything pertaining to running water) stems. We have already seen it in names such as Mersey and Hardy and modern O.S. Maps still identify Sale Ees and Ashton Ees. Because of the serious flood risk the use of the Meadows was generally restricted to hay and grazing but through to the end it was parcelled out so that every Chorlton farmer had a share. Additionally it served as a lung when Chorlton began to lose its fields to the builders and as a resort for the artisans of Manchester who wished to use their Sundays for the pursuit of illegal pastimes. It had the great advantage that on the arrival of the Lancashire Law they could slip across the Jackson's Boat Bridge to the safety of Cheshire Law.

The Meadows continued towards Northenden but for reasons which we need not discuss here, they were never as much used and most people taking the popular stroll to Northenden took the shorter field path past Barlow Hall to join the river bank near Red Bank Farm. This was the most extreme point of the Township and was often referred to as being a part of West Didsbury.

(Right top)
Haymaking on the Meadows field of farmer Higginbottom. It is not easy to offer a date but it is thought, from what the late Mr. Higginbottom said, to be about 1890.

(Right below)
The Back Lane or Hawthorn Lane near to the boundary with Stretford about 1890 and before the disposal of household refuse became a problem.

(Above and inset)

From the end of the footbridge ran the path that became Hardy Lane. This path has now gone, swallowed up by the Sports Field of U.M.I.S.T. Just before the path climbed up to the flood terrace was Hardy Lane Farm. In the traditional way of these things the public path went through the farmyard and the writer well remembers that one of the last tenants was always alert lest those passing through, particularly children, should exceed their rights of passage.

(Above left)

From the Old Village the usual approach was by way of Brook(burn) Road and over this little footbridge into the Boat Meadow. Again this scene is but a memory as is the meadow beyond.

(Left)

Hardy Lane was anything but the thoroughfare it is today. The only building, other than the farm already mentioned, was the large tenement building sometimes called the Block House.

(Right)
The edge of the flood plain is well illustrated here. The popular name for this spot was Bluebell Wood and each year it was a carpet of blue. Now it is engulfed by houses and the searcher, should he manage to locate the site, can count himself fortunate if he can find a dozen defiant blooms where once there were tens of thousands.
(Below left)
Red Bank Farm overlooks the river with the tower of Christ Church (in West Didsbury) in the background.
(Below right)
Park Eye was the tongue of farm land which was formed by the contortions of the river near to Red Bank Farm. It is a derivation of the Old English *ea* meaning an island and is used as a field name at several points along the river. When it became necessary to build a new road into north Cheshire it was the obvious site for an extension of Princess Road. This photograph shows the construction of the new road across the Eye with Christ Church tower, again, in the background.

Hough End

Although since 1641 Hough End was considered an administrative part of Withington, it was earlier a part of Chorlton and in the modern time has come back. For that reason, and the probability that it will otherwise be overlooked, it is dealt with here. In the main it was an open area drained by a number of small watercourses of which Chorlton Brook was the most important. The northern part was known as Jackson's Moss until Samuel Brooks developed it and bestowed on it the more euphemistic title of Whalley Range. The southerly area was part of Barlow Moor. The original Manor House of Withington was situated where Eddisbury Avenue is now but after the building of the new Hough End Hall for Sir Nicholas Mosley it became the site for Chorlton's Farm though the moat remained to the end.

(Left)

Nell Lane in the snow. This was the scene roughly where the Marist School now is. The original Royal Oak Inn was hereabouts.

(Below left)

Nell Lane looking north from the entrance to the courtyard in front of the Hall. Brookfield House (in Chorlton Park) is behind the trees. The view is one published by Renaud which makes it difficult to date since he used to re-issue old views. However the appearance of the bicycle suggests the date of about 1920.

(Below right)

Hough End Clough was in the past a popular open space. Now it has been restricted to the very narrow linear strip alongside the brook as the higher ground on each side has been appropriated for private use. At the far end was Twenty-Seven Steps, they just about remain!

(Above left)
This view shows the original Nell Lane Bridge, correctly it was Hough End Bridge, with the fields beyond which in time became Chorlton Park. The foreground, now built over, was in 1910 and later a favourite playground.

(Above right)
Manchester's first real aerodrome was on Hough End Fields. This view shows the hangars facing onto the railway to Stockport. The Greater Manchester County Police stables and dog training centre now stands on the site.

(Right)
A view along Wilbraham Road about 1913 or 1914. Just behind the tram is Woodlands Road and from here to St. Werburgh's Road was open country.

(Below)

The Dog House Farm was, as its name suggests, one of the farms which kennelled the hounds used by the Lord of the Manor for hunting. The farm, strictly the Old Dog House because there was a New Dog House Farm on Withington Lane, was sited where the pavilion of the Whalley Range Cricket Club stands now in Kingsbrook Road. One of the ancient footpaths of the district led directly from Hough End Hall to the farm.

(Bottom)

One of the roads to Manchester was by way of Moss Lane (part of it is now Sandy Lane and part White Moss Avenue) and a road roughly corresponding to today's Withington Road. On the White Moss Avenue part stood White Moss Farm and cottages. This part of Hough End was known as Nedd's Moss.

Manchester Road

Martledge

The part of the Township between, roughly, the railway and Longford Park and north of Wilbraham Road to Seymour Grove was Martledge. It was an area intersected by lazy streams that wandered from one pond to another and in a sort of inverted way it was known as the Isles. Apart from its use for farming it was exploited over the years as a source of clay for bricks and daub on the timber framed buildings. Initially the clay was extracted from open pits in the area now occupied by Oswald Road School etc. but when the building explosion occurred a major brick works developed at the bottom of Longford Road on the site now used by the school.

A large house called Sedge Lynn stood on Manchester Road. The outside wall and gatepost are recognisable on the early photograph which looks north from the end of Barlow Moor Road. The barns in the distance are those of Red Gate Farm and have now been replaced by the row of shops. The Library stands where the trees are to the left of the cart and the Billiard Hall is behind the bushes in the centre of the view. Sedge Lynn was demolished and eventually the site was used for the Savoy Cinema. After closure the cinema was converted into an undertaker's establishment.

(Below right)
The most northerly point of Chorlton was College Road where it meets Upper Chorlton Road. This early photograph, probably about 1895, shows a very different College Road from that of today.

(Opposite page)
Manchester Road curving away to meet Wilbraham Road. This part of the old main road to Manchester is now, except for a few yards at the Wilbraham Road end, the car park for the shopping precinct. The plot of land at the corner of Nicolas Road is advertised for sale – so see the next page . . .

(Below middle)
Sedge Lynn before Nicolas Road was built.

(Below left)
Probably the view of Sedge Lynn would not be very important were it not for the remarkable pair of views which the occupier, Mr. Booth, photographed on the 8th November, 1882. The one reproduced here, taken from a back bedroom window, shows the wide desolate expanse of the Isles with nothing between the house and Longford Hall. The light covering of snow emphasises the few trees and hedges that existed.

Manley Hall

Samuel Mendel was an emigree from Russia who established a thriving export business around the middle of last century. The house he built was located on the edge of the later boundary of the Township approximately where Manley Park is.

The house cost £120,000 to build and its collection of works of art was reputed to be the finest in the North of England. The opening of the Suez Canal altered completely the pattern of trade on which Sam's success was built and he had to sell the Hall, its contents, carriages, horses etc. and died a ruined man in 1894.

There were proposals for using the house but these finally foundered as the result of a grandiose scheme to turn it into the Manley Hall Winter Garden Society Ltd. and early in this century it was demolished.

(Left)
Manley Hall about 1890 after the neglect resulting from its sale and future uncertainty had begun to show. A well-known view from the same viewpoint shows what it was like in its heyday.
(Below)
The rear view of the Hall in 1904. The decay and effects of demolition are evident.

Wilbraham Road stretched away towards Stretford. It ended, officially, where it met Edge Lane but for many years its private character was indicated by a gate positioned at the end of Maidstone Avenue. Before Wilbraham Road was built Edge Lane was joined by Cow Lane which gave access to the Isles. The final bend in Wilbraham Road was probably dictated by the desire to avoid Cow Lane having to be accommodated in the new road. Cow Lane still existed in part until very recently though Hampton Road had been built out of its Edge Lane end.

(Above left and right)
Wilbraham Road about 1910. The hut in the roadway in the centre distance was the cabby's hut though it is thought to have earlier been the fire post which was situated hereabouts. The trees which are now a feature of the road have not yet been planted.

(Right, Cow Lane)

(Right)
Chorltonville owed its inception to James Herbert Dawson. He retired to Lytham St. Annes and was actively engaged in local politics there. This photograph was taken when he was First Citizen of that Council.

(Below)
After the completion of the 'ville there were visits from the photographers of the major publishers of picture postcards. On the day of this visit he attracted the attention of a little girl with a tennis racket. She seems to have followed him round and posed on most of the views he took. The date is 1912/13 and the privet hedges have barely started to show themselves.

Chorltonville

One of the features of Chorlton is the garden estate of Chorltonville. Whilst not the oldest of this type of development it does merit inclusion in the story of urban housing.

The estate was the brainchild of two members of the congregation of the Cavendish Chapel at All Saints. James Herbert Dawson was a Manchester draper and William John Vowles a boot and shoe salesman who hailed from the south.

It was the intention of these two visionaries to provide better homes for those who lived in such unsalubrious areas as Hulme and Chorlton-on-Medlock but things did not turn out as envisaged and Chorltonville became one of the most desirable residential areas. In their promotions they were joined by Thomas Whitely as builder (he had already built the Cavendish (now Corkland) Road estate and together they established Darley Hall Estate Ltd. and purchased the Darley Hall estate of Reuben Spencer. This small area at West Point was wholly in the Stretford Urban District Council's area and the shops which face the Seymour Hotel (as it now is) were the only commercial properties they were ever involved in. Lindow Road off Seymour Grove can be recognised as the embryo of Chorltonville. This project was successfully completed in 1908 and encouraged a more ambitious scheme and so the 'Ville was projected and officially opened with due ceremony in 1911. The estate was provided with its own social amenities in the form of tennis courts, a bowling green and a children's playground.

Chorltonville was another success story and so further encouraged, the three decided to build an even bigger estate at Polefield, Prestwich. Only a small part of this third project had been completed when war broke out in 1914 and stopped all further work. After the war, conditions were so changed that it was necessary to disband the three companies which administered the estates and the properties were sold off to the sitting tenants where they wished to buy.

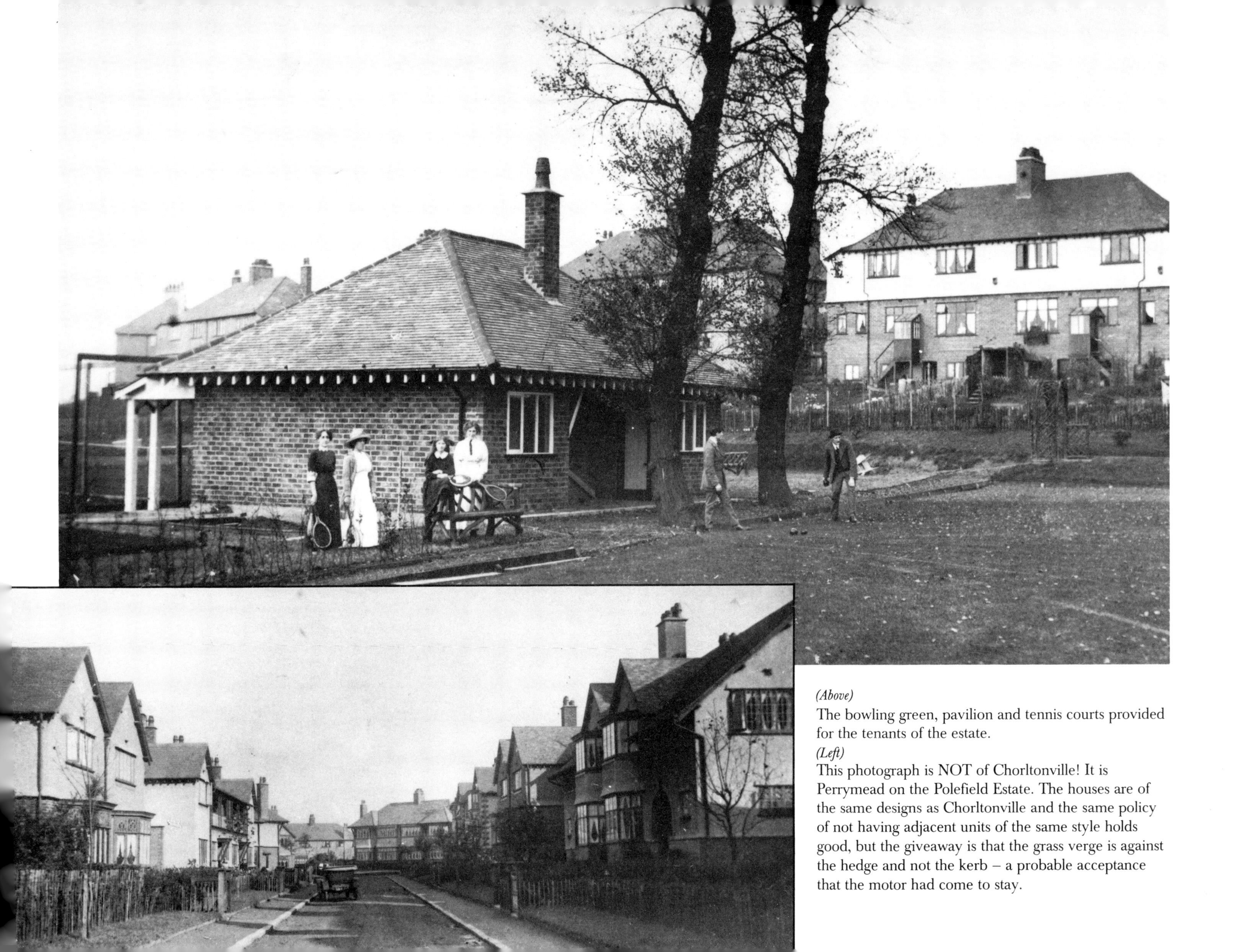

(Above)
The bowling green, pavilion and tennis courts provided for the tenants of the estate.
(Left)
This photograph is NOT of Chorltonville! It is Perrymead on the Polefield Estate. The houses are of the same designs as Chorltonville and the same policy of not having adjacent units of the same style holds good, but the giveaway is that the grass verge is against the hedge and not the kerb – a probable acceptance that the motor had come to stay.

(Left middle)
A view of West Point about 1905. The constable was shot by the wall on the right. Through the trees (where the shops now are) can be seen the roof of Darley Hall which, it is thought, was Peace's target on the fateful night.

(Left bottom)
Another photograph of West Point but this time 14th March 1924 (!). The blue bricks which were inserted in the wall to mark where the bullet lodged were behind the lamp-post. Behind the wall is the home of Samuel Gratrix which now, extended by a mirror image, is the Seymour Hotel.

Chorlton's Major Crime

Charles Peace, lame and vain, was a petty thief, rogue and much given to a false opinion of his attractiveness to women. He was in the habit of travelling from where he was currently living, to houses at considerable distances away and thoroughly 'casing' them before the burglary.

He was often active in Manchester and on 1st August 1876 while walking down Upper Chorlton Road to the house he had previously selected as his objective, he aroused the suspicions of P.C.'s Cock and Beanland. P.C. Cock separated from his companion in order to follow Peace and on surprising the latter at the end of Seymour Grove he received a pistol shot in the chest from which he died.

Suspicion for the killing at first fell on the two Habron brothers. They were agricultural workers who had come to the notice of the police on account of their poaching activities. In the Royal Oak Inn they had been heard to say that they would get even with Cock who, it would seem, was a particularly zealous officer. William, aged 18, was found guilty but fortunately the death sentence was not imposed so that when Peace was apprehended on another charge and confessed to this killing, justice could be done.

Police Constable Nicholas Cock was buried in the Old Church yard and the Lancashire Police erected a magnificent headstone to his grave. With the closure of the Old Church the stone was transferred to the Police Headquarters at Preston 1956 and it now stands on the side of the main drive.

(Top left)
The headstone and grave of P. C. Nicholas Cock in the Old Churchyard.

(Middle)
For obvious reasons Peace shunned photographs of himself. This is, so far as is known, the only authentic photograph and is from the 'Ticket of Leave' book by courtesy of the South Yorkshire Police.